THE POETIC GARDEN
of
LIU ZONGYUAN

LIU ZONGYUAN

柳宗元 著

THE POETIC GARDEN
of LIU ZONGYUAN

柳宗元花苑

TRANSLATED BY

Nathaniel Dolton-Thornton
& *Yu Yuanyuan*

杜尚楠 于元元 译

With a preface by Robert Hass

PHONEME
MEDIA

DEEP
VELLUM

DALLAS, TEXAS

Phoneme Media, an imprint of Deep Vellum Publishing
3000 Commerce St., Dallas, Texas 75226

Deep Vellum is a 501c3 nonprofit literary arts organization founded in 2013 with the mission to bring the world into conversation through literature.

Support for this publication has been provided in part by grants from Anhui University, the National Endowment for the Arts, the Texas Commission on the Arts, the City of Dallas Office of Arts and Culture, and the George and Fay Young Foundation.

ISBNS: 978-1-64605-217-2 (trade paperback) | 978-1-64605-243-1 (ebook)

LIBRARY OF CONGRESS CONTROL NUMBER
2023020026

Cataloging-in-Publication data is available.

Details from the painting *Fishing Alone on the Cold River* (2013) appear by permission of the artist, Zhao Chunqiu.

The other images that appear in the book are *Two Egrets in a Willow Pond* by Huang Shen (1687–1772), "Ascending Liuzhou's Gate Tower: A Poem to the Prefects of Zhangzhou, Tingzhou, Fengzhou, and Lianzhou," calligraphy believed to be by Liu Zongyuan, and *Pine and Plum* by Pan Tianshou (1897–1971).

Cover design by Nick Motte
Interior layout and typesetting by Kit Schluter

PRINTED IN THE UNITED STATES OF AMERICA

Contents[1]

Interlude (815)
[幕间 (815)]

PART TWO: *Liuzhou* (815–819)
[二、柳州 (815–819)]

Preface: Meeting Liu Zongyuan

ROBERT HASS

I FIRST BECAME AWARE OF LIU ZONGYUAN WHEN NATHANIEL Dolton-Thornton appeared at my office hours in the upper reaches of Wheeler Hall at the University of California at Berkeley. I had been teaching a workshop on the translation of poetry, which I assume is what brought Nathaniel to me. He was, he explained, an environmental science major who was also studying classical Chinese, and he had begun to make translations of this Tang Dynasty poet in part because he was attracted to Liu Zongyuan's botanical specificity. He had written a lot of poems about gardening. I was, of course, fascinated, and Nathaniel began to visit my office weekly with new poems, so that after a while it felt as if, along with Nathaniel, Liu Zongyuan with his steady gaze and haunted calm was visiting my office every week. Reading the poems, I thought about what I knew of Liu Zongyuan's world. I saw that he belonged to the generation after Li Bai (Li Po) and Du Fu (Tu Fu), the Tang poets most Western readers know, and thought that his poems shared with the poets of that time an ideal of calm, at least of self-cultivation, in a violent and unstable world. I thought also of the Roman poet Ovid and his *Tristia*, the classic book of exile in the Western tradition. And Czeslaw Milosz's *City Without a Name*. They were poems that resonated in many ways.

Nathaniel went on to do graduate work at Cambridge University and met Yu Yuanyuan, who had come from China to study modern English and American poetry, in a workshop. It is a great gift that they have been able to complete the work that Nathaniel had begun and have brought the world of Liu Zongyuan alive for English readers. In doing so, they were entering a powerful literary tradition. The great

XI

poets of the Tang Dynasty entered the bloodstream of poetry in the English language a little more than a hundred years ago in 1915, when Ezra Pound published *Cathay*, a small book of the reworked notes on the translations of some of the poems of Li Bai, sent to Pound by the widow of Ernest Fenellosa. Three years later Arthur Waley published *A Hundred and Seventy Chinese Poems*, which introduced Bai Juyi (Po Chu-i) to English readers. What followed was, for English-language poets and readers, the discovery of China. In 1921 Amy Lowell and the Sinologist Florence Ayscough published *Fir-Flower Tablets: Poems Translated from the Chinese*, adding Du Fu and Wang Wei to the Tang poets introduced to Western readers. In 1918 Witter Bynner, who had been Wallace Stevens's classmate at Harvard and was teaching at the University of California at Berkeley, met Jiang Kanghu (Kiang Kang-hu), who had been brought to the university to start an East Asian languages department. Bynner had just returned from a trip to China and teamed up with Professor Jiang to produce *The Jade Mountain:Three Hundred Poems from the T'ang Dynasty*, published in 1929.

From this distance this sudden jolt of interest in a three-millennium-old literary tradition about which most English and American readers were entirely ignorant doesn't seem so surprising, nor does the fact that the exploration of East Asian poetry became a critical element in the development of the modernist aesthetic. Consider Arthur Waley on the translation of Chinese poems:

> Most of the poems in this book are either in five syllables or in lines of seven syllables all the way through. In the English, so far as possible, a stress represents each syllable; so that a Chinese reader will easily recognize the meter of the original. I have not used rhyme, because what is really in the long run of most interest to English readers is what the poems say; and if one uses rhyme, it is impossible not to sacrifice sense to sound. For the same reason I have chosen poems which say something interesting. Those are the ones that translate best. It does not at all follow that they rank highest as poetry in the original, but with very few exceptions the poems in this book are by poets whom the Chinese themselves have always greatly admired.

So, in order to translate these rhymed and metrical poems, Pound and Waley took the rhyme and meter out—at just the moment, in the middle of the 1910s, when young English and American poets were trying to figure out what their poetry might sound like if they took the rhyme and meter out. The work of Pound and Waley showed a way, one that placed front and center the declarative sentence and the syntax of the English language, and it did so at a moment when the young poets in London in the Imagist group were also interested in directness of presentation. Pound was working from Ernest Fenellosa's notes on the poems and his essay on the Chinese language, in which he argued that Chinese characters were pictorial in origin, represented actions or, placed next to one another, the action of metaphor, of the new thought created by a suddenly perceived similarity between disparate objects, and were therefore closer representations of reality and of the way the mind works than the abstracted nouns, the generalizing intelligence, in European languages. Whether this was true of Chinese or not, it spoke very directly to the poets trying to forge a new idiom in English. Pound got Fenellosa's essay published in a literary magazine, and it became one of the documents of the new poetry, so that, years later, in the next generation, Muriel Rukeyser in her 1949 *The Life of Poetry* would turn to Fenellosa to describe her own aesthetic. "The type of the sentence in nature," Fenellosa wrote, "is a flash of lightning. It passes between two terms, a cloud and the earth."

Reading that now, one gets a sense of just how electric those first translations seemed to their new readers. Most of the Chinese lyrics— five- or seven-character poems, as Waley observed—begin with the description of either a setting or a state of mind. Many of the opening lines of Pound's versions still carry that charge:

> The jeweled steps are already quite white with dew

> While my hair was still cut straight across my forehead,
> I played about the front gate, picking flowers

Pound reports working with Waley and urging him to use an English syntax as natural as possible. The effect, whether it originated in Waley or Pound or Bai Juyi, was to give the tenor of that poet a sense of levelheaded calm.

> In waters still as a burnished mirror's face,
> In the depths of Wei, carp and grayling swim.

And with the pleasures of the declarative sentence came the pleasure of the interrogative one:

> Illness and idleness give me much leisure.
> What do I do with leisure when it comes?

This method became the idiom of classical Chinese poetry throughout the twentieth century. Among the poets, Kenneth Rexroth gave American readers their Du Fu with *100 Poems from the Chinese* in 1956, and Gary Snyder brought forth *Cold Mountain Poems*, a translation of the monk and hermit Han Shan, in 1959.

A generation of scholars and translators deepened this access. David Hawkes, a British scholar mentored by Arthur Waley, produced *Ch'u Tzu: Songs of the South* in 1959 and *A Little Primer of Tu Fu* in 1967. The American scholar Burton Watson published versions of Su Shi (Su Dongpo or Su Tung-Po) and Du Fu and a version of the writings of Zhuangzi (Chuang Tzu) for readers who wanted to get a sense of the Taoist sensibility in Tang poetry. In the next generation two American poet translators, David Hinton and Red Pine, added to the mix. Hinton published *Selected Poems of Du Fu* in 1989 and *Selected Poems of Li Po* in 1996. Red Pine, nom de plume of the independent scholar Bill Porter, gave us a number of works by different poets, most recently *Written in Exile: The Poetry of Liu Tsung-yuan* (Liu Zongyuan) in 2019. It is in this tradition that Nathaniel Dolton-Thornton and Yu Yuanyuan have worked so effectively in giving us their Liu Zongyuan.

In the fifty years since *Cathay*, Western readers went from more or less complete ignorance of Chinese literature to, among the poets, understanding that a little familiarity with the work of Du Fu, Li Bai, Wang Wei, Bai Juyi, Han Shan, and Su Shi was as fundamental to a poet's education as knowledge of classical Greek or Roman poetry or the work of Shakespeare or Baudelaire. And the attraction of Chinese poetry was not only formal and aesthetic. The young poets at the outset of the twentieth century were not only engaged in a renovation of their art; most of them were looking to revalue the values of their culture. In his introduction to *The Jade Mountain* Witter Bynner wrote: "Like most of us who have been schooled in this Western world, I was afforded, in my youth, a study of culture flowing from two sources, the Greek and the Hebrew." And, he writes, "I have come by accident into as close touch with Chinese poetry as a westerner is able to come without knowledge of the Chinese tongue. And I feel with conviction that in the matter of poetry I have begun to receive a new, finer, and deeper education than ever came to me from the Hebrew or the Greek." This impulse figured in Pound's attraction to Confucius (whom he referred to as Kung, de-Latinizing his name) and in Arthur Waley's *Three Ways of Thought in Ancient China*, a sense that absorbing the Chinese poets meant absorbing something of the Confucian, Taoist, and Buddhist contexts of their world.

The Poetic Garden of Liu Zongyuan joins Red Pine's *Written in Exile* in bringing Liu Zongyuan's poems into the English-language canon, even perhaps making it for new readers of the poetry of this time a good place to start. The tension between Confucian modes of engagement and balance and a Taoist or Buddhist cultivation, usually troubled, of an inner life. A brilliant courtier and administrator as a young man, a troubled exile who turns to the natural world and the garden in his later years, he seems—in the generation after Li Bai and Du Fu—to gather to himself and revise many of the themes of the Chinese lyric, so it is a gift to receive this version of the poems from a new generation of collaborative translators with an eye that is both environmental and alert to literary traditions.

As for Liu Zongyuan, his best-known poem, four lines long, twenty characters, could be said to be a complete expression of what attracted Western readers to Chinese art. "Chinese poetry," Witter Bynner wrote, "rarely trespassed beyond the bounds of actuality." Its gift, he claims, is to name the human condition as it is. One could make this claim for Liu Zongyuan's "River Snow." Here is the Dolton-Thornton and Yu version:

RIVER SNOW

No bird hovers above a thousand hills.
No footprint remains on ten thousand trails.
One boat: an old man in a straw raincoat
is fishing alone in cold river snow.

—*Nathaniel Dolton-Thornton*
and Yu Yuanyuan

And here, to give you a sense of the way the tradition has encountered and absorbed this remarkably simple poem, is a little history of its translation:

RIVER SNOW

XVI

A hundred mountains and no bird,
A thousand paths without a footprint;
A little boat, a bamboo cloak,
An old man fishing in the cold river-snow

—*Witter Bynner*

RIVER SNOW

(5-ch *chueh-chu*)

From a thousand hills, bird flights have vanished;
on ten thousand paths, human traces wiped out:
lone boat, an old man in straw cape and hat,
fishing alone in the cold river snow.

—*Burton Watson*

RIVER SNOW

These thousand peaks cut off the flight of birds
On all the trails, human tracks are gone
A single boat—coat—hat—an old man!
Alone fishing chill river snow.

—*Gary Snyder*

RIVER SNOW

A thousand mountains and not a bird flying
Ten thousand paths and not a single footprint
An old man in a raincoat in a solitary boat
Fishes alone in the freezing river snow

—RED PINE

RIVER SNOW

Mountains—

No birds arise

Footpaths—

Run
Out

Of

Footprints

Lone boat—

Straw cloak/
Bamboo hats

Man

Seen

Casting

Cold river snow

—MAY WONG

A reader could do worse than start here to think about the nature of translation, the particular teasing magic of "River Snow," and the human condition.

Bynner, Witter and Kiang Kang-Hu, translators. *The Jade Mountain*. New York: Knopf, 1929.

Liu, Tsung-Yuan. *Written in Exile: Poems of Liu Tsung-Yuan*, translated by Red Pine. Port Townsend, WA: Copper Canyon, 2019.

Snyder, Gary, translator. In *The New Directions Book of Classical Chinese Poetry*, edited by Eliot Weinberger. New York: New Directions, 2003.

Watson, Burton, editor. *The Columbia Book of Classical Chinese Poetry*. New York: Columbia University Press, 1984.

Wong, May, translator. *In the Same Light: 200 Poems for our Century from the Migrants and Exiles of the Tang Dynasty*. Brooklyn: The Song Cave, 2022.

Introduction

NATHANIEL DOLTON-THORNTON & YU YUANYUAN

IN AUGUST OF 805 CE, COURT EUNUCHS IN THE TANG DYNASTY [唐朝] (618–907) capital at Chang'an [长安] ended the six-month rule of high-ranking official Wang Shuwen's [王叔文] (753–806) political reform group. Shortly afterward, the new emperor, Xianzong [唐宪宗] (r. 805–820), exiled ten of the group's key members. Among them was thirty-two-year-old Liu Zongyuan [柳宗元]² (773–819), the politically ambitious descendant of a declining aristocratic family. Recognized in Chang'an as something of a child prodigy, Liu had passed the highest imperial exam (becoming a *jinshi* [进士]) at only twenty years old. From an early age, he was widely regarded as a literary master, and people from near and far visited him to receive tutoring, articles, poems, or even a few brief lines of writing. Together with Han Yu [韩愈] (768–824), Liu led the burgeoning Classical (*Guwen* [古文]) Movement, which advocated clear, concise, structurally simple, and relatively free writing (which had been popular before the Jin Dynasty [晋朝], 266–420), often for social, moral, and political ends. At the same time, Liu rose quickly through the ranks of the central government. But when the reform movement failed, Liu was sent a thousand miles away to Yongzhou [永州] Prefecture in modern South China's Hunan Province. Except for a brief month in Chang'an in 815, Liu would spend the rest of his life as a demoted official on the southern margins of the Chinese empire: first in Yongzhou Prefecture (805–815), then farther south in Liuzhou [柳州] Prefecture, modern Guangxi Province (815–819). Trapped in an alien landscape, Liu went on to write many prose and verse pieces in the Guwen style, almost all of them imbued with the environment of South China or the experience of exile, as well as Liu's flickering (but never extinguished) political ambition. Though Liu died in exile, through his writings he secured a place for himself in Chinese history—something he had failed to do in politics—one deeply intertwined with the landscapes of South China. Song Dynasty [宋朝] (960–1279) author and critic Su Shi [苏轼] (1037–1101) writes of Liu's poetry:

> Following Li Bo [Li Bai] and Du Fu, poets continued to appear, but while they had fine taste, their talent did not match their intent. Only Wei Yingwu [韦应物] and Liu Zongyuan produced delicate profusion through the simple and the old, and brought out consummate flavor from the flat and the plain:[3] a feat which no others could attain.[4]

Elsewhere, Su Shi describes Liu's poems as "lean outside while rich inside; plain in appearance yet delicious when tasted,"[5] and "mild, beautiful, peaceful, and profound."[6] Liu's prose writing has also received high praise. By the Ming Dynasty (1368–1644), Liu (along with both Han Yu and Su Shi) was listed as one of the "Eight Prose Masters of the Tang and Song" (*Tang Song badajia* [唐宋八大家]). His name is still familiar among the classical writers read and studied in China today, with his essays and poems (such as "River Snow" [《江雪》] and "Old Fisherman" [《渔翁》], both included in this collection) appearing in school textbooks at multiple levels.

English-language critics have also appreciated Liu's writings. They have often focused on his prose,[7] such as his "travel records" (*youji* [游记]), in which he describes hikes to scenic landscapes around his home in South China. Several of his most famous poems (especially "River Snow") have been anthologized and translated multiple times. However, the rest of his poetry has received less attention. In part, this might be because Liu wrote relatively few poems—about 160—while better-known poets such as Du Fu [杜甫] (712–770), Li Bai [李白] (701–762), and Bai Juyi [白居易] (772–846) left over one thousand poems. Until now, only one book dedicated to English translations of Liu's poetry exists: Red Pine's *Written in Exile: The Poetry of Liu Tsung-Yuan* (2019).

Representing the joint work of two translators (one Chinese and one American), *The Poetic Garden of Liu Zongyuan* aims to further introduce

Liu's excellent poems on South China's plants and landscapes to the English-speaking world. We've found ourselves drawn especially to Liu's remarkable poems on South China's landscapes because, besides being vivid, they're also unusual. Among the most noteworthy of these pieces are what we've come to call Liu's "plant poems." Each of these poems includes a sustained reflection on a plant. The pieces frequently relate to the established style of "poems on things" (*yongwu* [咏物]), in which a described object often metonymically reflects the speaker's thoughts, feelings, or aspirations. Various poets wrote yongwu-style poems on plants in the Tang Dynasty, but few wrote as many high-quality pieces as did Liu. Moreover, unlike most other poets who wrote "plant poems," Liu was more than simply an admirer of plants; he was also a gardener, interested in the details of plants' habitats, requirements, and specific uses. This focus is most evident in his distinctive "planting poems," which are especially uncommon in the context of Chinese-language poetry. Many of these poems are titled with the same formula, *zhong* [种] ("to sow, to seed, to plant") followed by a plant species' name. Of the over 2,200 poets anthologized in the *Complete Tang Poems* (*Quan Tangshi* [《全唐诗》]), only Bai Juyi wrote more poems with "种" in their titles (fifteen) than did Liu (seven). (Taking into account two more terms for planting, *zai* [栽] and *zhi* [植], Liu wrote fourteen such poems.) Given that Bai left about 2,800 extant poems, more than any earlier poet, while Liu left only 160, Liu's focus on planting poems is especially striking.

Perhaps even more remarkable are the species Liu chooses to write about, some of which appear nowhere else in the more than forty thousand poems of the *Complete Tang Poems*. Some are also absent from or scarce in the Liang Dynasty (502–587) *Selections of Refined Literature* (*Wen Xuan* [《文选》]), compiled by Xiao Tong [萧统] (501–531), as well as the *Tang Dynasty Collection of Literature Arranged by Categories* (*Yiwen Leiju* [《艺文类聚》]), compiled by Ouyang Xun [欧阳询] (557–641). Many other Tang poets who write about planting do so in general terms, or name one of several popular plant types: trees (*shu* [树]), flowers (*hua* [花]), willows (*liu* [柳]), and bamboo (*zhu* [竹]) are some of the most common subjects. In contrast, Liu's planting poems include white myoga ginger (*bai rang he* [白蘘荷]) (*Zingiber mioga*), fairy wings (*xian ling pi* [仙灵毗]) (*Epimedium* sp.), *bai zhu* (*zhu* [术]) (likely *Atractylodes macrocephala*), the "tree of longevity" (*ling shou mu* [灵寿木]) (possibly a *Viburnum* sp.), noble dendrobium (*mu hu* [木斛]) (*Dendrobium nobile*), and banyan (*rong* [榕]) (likely *Ficus microcarpa*). With so few poetic references, these marginal plants aren't as tightly yoked to the associations formed by earlier literary references as are cultural heavyweights like plum (*mei* [梅]) and pine (*song* [松]), which occur one thousand times and over three thousand times respectively in the *Complete Tang Poems*. Liu's decision to focus on marginal plants with little poetic precedent suggests, among other things, the importance of his persistent attention to features of the landscape itself—as he finds and modifies it—to the composition of his poems.

Liu's interest in the material specifics of South China's landscapes reappears throughout his "planting poems." For instance, in the early poem "Planting White Myoga Ginger" [种白蘘荷], he reflects on the physical habits and medicinal benefits of the piece's titular plant. The plant's two-character name, *ranghe* [蘘荷], appears only twice in the *Complete Tang Poems* anthology: in one instance, it happens to be the proper name of a pavilion; the other is Liu's poem. Liu opens his piece with a reference to a supposed custom in some regions that involved converting "lower animal life" (called the *gu* [蛊] insect) into poison.[8] After describing his physical and emotional suffering in his new home, Liu turns to his source of relief: a local species, white myoga ginger. A shade-loving plant native to China, myoga ginger has a long history of medicinal use. It is mentioned in the *Records of the Rites of Zhou* (*Zhouli* [《周礼》]), probably written around 200 BCE, as a valuable cure (along with "conjuring spells") for internal parasites. In his *Records of the Grand Historian* (*Shiji* [《史记》]), Sima Qian [司马迁] (145–86 BCE) even mentions myoga ginger as effective specifically for "managing the *gu* insect poison" 「治蛊毒也」.[9] Liu recognizes both white myoga ginger's growth preferences ("It thrives in an emerald tree's shade") and its medicinal uses ("I rely on it for my well-being"). Here, Liu transfers place- and plant-specific knowledge from prose into verse to create a remarkable piece of poetry.

To give one more example: in "Planting the Tree of Longevity" (also written in Yongzhou), Liu focuses on a plant that occurs in literature even less frequently than white myoga ginger. Liu's poem is the tree of longevity's only mention in the entire *Complete Tang Poems* anthology, and the plant is absent from the *Selections of Refined Literature*. As in "Planting White Myoga Ginger," in this poem Liu attends closely to the specifics of his subject's physical characteristics and uses. The tree of longevity has been tentatively identified as a *Viburnum* species, which Liu's poem seems to affirm.[10] He describes the plant in detail, including its "pliant stem" and "strong nodes [that] often appear opposite one another." In line with Liu's account, *Viburnum* species are renowned for having straight and pliant stems.

Liu also reflects on the tree of longevity's uses. Line seven ("How could I hope for the honor of an Elder's Cane?") alludes to the tradition of creating honorary canes for elders from the tree. For instance, the *History of the Former Han Dynasty* (Han shu [《汉书》], completed III CE) mentions a story in which the empress dowager recognizes the aged imperial tutor Kong Guang [孔光] by bestowing on him a "cane of longevity" 「灵寿杖」. As the third-century-CE commentator Meng Kang [孟康] glosses, the term refers to a "staff for supporting an old person" 「扶老杖也」.[11] At first, Liu seems to regret that his exile, or "limping" along in the south (which could refer to the thiamine deficiency he'd developed in Yongzhou or more general physical or emotional suffering), prevents him from contributing enough to his country to receive an Elder's Cane. But toward the poem's end his description takes a turn: as he touches the living plant, he says, he can "forget [his] fatigue" and "feel a spring in [his] step." Visiting his South China garden, sharing the space with a growing tree of longevity (which satisfies his "desire for wilderness"), Liu finds himself restored to life. Like the plant, Liu realizes, he doesn't need formal recognition to be well. "How could I possibly cut it down / and use it to lean on while walking?" he concludes. Here and elsewhere, Liu acknowledges and explores the characteristics and uses of the plants he finds in South China, tightening their relationship to Chinese poetry even as he plays with—and occasionally rejects—their traditional connotations. While the poems often reflect his feelings and aspirations, Liu always pays close attention to the plants themselves, the plants he can touch, the plants he lives with in the South China landscape that is his final home.

Translating Classical Chinese poetry into English presents several challenges. To begin with, as many writers and critics have said, exact duplication from one language to another is impossible. We agree, but we also like Charles Simic's thoughts on the matter: "Even in this claim that to translate poetry is impossible, I find an ideal situation. Poetry itself is about the impossible. All arts are about doing the impossible. That's their attraction." Second, there are some major formal differences between Classical Chinese and most English-language poetry. Like much Classical Chinese poetry, Liu's original poems usually have a strict number of characters per line (often five or seven), end rhymes,

and no punctuation. In terms of punctuation, we initially experimented with leaving punctuation out of our translations but decided to include it for clarity, which aligns with the common practice in modern Chinese textbooks. In terms of metrical structures and rhyme schemes, we've tried to strike a balance among meaning, sound, and meter. Most English-language translators have opted to translate Classical Chinese poetry into free verse. We recognize the value of this approach, but, in our translations, we also want to acknowledge in some way the pattern of the original Chinese poems. To that end, our translations are in free verse but contain a number of beats per line roughly equal to the number of characters per line in the Chinese original. (For instance, we try to translate a five-character, pentasyllabic Chinese poem into an English poem with around four to six beats per line.) This pattern aims to echo, without directly replicating, the Chinese form. It's also in tune with T. S. Eliot's observation in "Reflections On *Vers Libre*": "The most interesting verse which has yet been written in our language has been done either by taking a very simple form, like the iambic pentameter, and constantly withdrawing from it, or taking no form at all, and constantly approximating to a very simple one." That said, we prioritize attention to the Chinese text's meaning. Where we feel the language requires it, we allow lines to run shorter or longer. Where Liu uses end rhyme, we use internal rhyme and slant rhyme to gesture toward Liu's practice without sacrificing accuracy in meaning. Our translation of Liu's "River Snow," in which Liu uses an AABA rhyme scheme, exemplifies our approach:

> No bird hovers above a thousand hills.
> No footprint remains on ten thousand trails.
> One boat: an old man in a straw raincoat
> is fishing alone in cold river snow.

千山鸟飞绝
万径人踪灭
孤舟蓑笠翁
独钓寒江雪

Chinese pronunciation in pinyin form:

QIĀN SHĀN NIǍO FĒI JUÉ
WÀN JÌNG RÉN ZŌNG MIÈ
GŪ ZHŌU SUŌ LÌ WĒNG
DÚ DIÀO HÁN JIĀNG XUĚ

——NATHANIEL DOLTON-THORNTON & YU YUANYUAN

1. Some titles in the contents are abbreviated. Our abbreviations follow those in the *Collected Works of Liu Hedong* [《柳河东集》], the oldest collection of Liu Zongyuan's writings, which was compiled by his friend, the poet Liu Yuxi [刘禹锡] (772–842) around 819–821.

2. Liu Zongyuan has also been called Liu Zihou [柳子厚], Liu Hedong [柳河东], and Liu Liuzhou [柳柳州], among other names.

3. For more on the aesthetic of "*blandness*" (*pingdan* [平淡]) and its place in the Chinese literary tradition, see François Jullien's *Éloge de la fadeur* (translated by Paula Varsano as *In Praise of Blandness*) and Paula Varsano, "The Invisible Landscape of Wei Yingwu (737–792)," *Harvard Journal of Asiatic Studies* 54, no. 2 (December 1994), 407–435.

4. William H. Nienhauser et al., *Liu Tsung-Yüan* (Woodbridge, CT: Twayne, 1973), 255, 91. We have changed proper names from the Wade-Giles spellings used in Neinhauser's translation to the pinyin equivalents.

5. From Su Shi's essay "Comment on the Poems by Han Yu and Liu Zongyuan" [《评韩柳诗》] in the *Collected Works of Su Shi* [《苏轼文集》], ed. Kong Fanli (Beijing: Zhonghua Book Company, 1986), 2109–2110.

6. *Ibid.*

7. Engaging discussions of Liu's prose writings can be found in books such as Ao Wang's *Spatial Imaginaries in Mid-Tang China* (Amherst, NY: Cambria Press, 2018), Stephen Owen's *The End of the Chinese 'Middle Ages': Essays in Mid-Tang Literary Culture* (Stanford: Stanford University Press, 1996), and Anna Shields's *One Who Knows Me: Friendship and Literary Culture in Mid-Tang China* (Leiden, Netherlands: Brill Academic Publishers, 2020).

8. See note 27 to "Planting White Myoga Ginger" for the details of this practice.

9. Sima Qian [司马迁], *Records of the Grand Historian* [《史记》]. Cited in Wang Guo'an [王国安], *Liu Zongyuan Shi Jian Shi* [《柳宗元诗笺释》], 227.

10. Peter K. Bol, *"This Culture of Ours": Intellectual Transitions in T'ang and Sung China* (Stanford: Stanford University Press, 1992), 143. Paul W. Kroll, *A Student's Dictionary of Classical and Medieval Chinese* (Leiden, Netherlands: Brill Academic Publishers, 2017), 223. The entry is for 「椐」. E. Bretschneider notes that 「椐」 and 「灵寿木」 are synonymous. See E. Bretschneider, *Botanicon Sinicum: Notes on Chinese Botany from Native and Western Sources: Part 2, The Botany of the Chinese Classics* (Shanghai: Kelly & Walsh, Limited., 1892).

11. Ban Gu [班固]; Ban Zhao [班昭], "Kong Guang's Biography" in the *History of the Former Han Dynasty* [《汉书·孔光传》]. Cited in *ibid*, 114.

PART ONE: *Yongzhou* (805–815)

I N THE WINTER OF 805, LIU ZONGYUAN ARRIVED in Yongzhou to serve as a minor official. Finding himself houseless, he took up residence in two local Buddhist temples, Longxing Temple and Fahua Temple. He befriended the heads of both temples, as he expresses in "A Poem Composed in Return for the Reverent Monk Xun's Gift, the Fresh Tea He Gathered from among Bamboo" [《酬巽上人以竹间自采新茶见赠》]. Liu found life in Yongzhou very difficult. His mother died soon after they arrived in the area. His friends and connections in the north seemed to have abandoned him. Moreover, with few official duties, Liu had no way to realize his political ambitions. He soon developed thiamine deficiency, a condition common among northerners exiled to the south. The condition weakened his legs and, eventually, contributed to his death in Liuzhou in 819. However, in late 808, Liu's symptoms subsided.

Over time, Liu explored Yongzhou's distinct landscape. In his poetry and prose from this period, he reflects on his discoveries and his complex relationship with his new home. He describes plants that are rarely if ever mentioned in Chinese poetry, such as white myoga ginger and the tree of longevity, as well as climate phenomena distinct to South China, such as the plum rain season. Eventually, he set up residence beside Ran

Creek, a stream he discovered on one of his hikes in the region, and set about cultivating the surrounding landscape. While still a rising official in Chang'an, Liu had received high praise for his writing. As Liu's friend Han Yu writes, "He won fame immediately. Out of admiration, people were eager to make his acquaintance."[1] But it was in Yongzhou that Liu's literary talent, sparked by suffering and nurtured by imposed leisure, short journeys, and painful meditation, reached its height. Readers today can still glimpse Liu's remarkable life through this poetic garden.

巽上人以竹间自采新茶见赠，酬之以诗

芳丛翳湘竹
零露凝清华
复此雪山客
晨朝掇灵芽
蒸烟俯石濑
咫尺凌丹崖
圆方丽奇色
圭璧无纤瑕
呼儿爨金鼎
馀馥延幽遐
涤虑发真照
还源荡昏邪
犹同甘露饭
佛事熏毗耶
咄此蓬瀛侣
无乃贵流霞

A Poem Composed in Return for the Reverent Monk Xun's Gift, the Fresh Tea He Gathered from among Bamboo[2]

Xiang bamboo[3] shades a fragrant thicket
where pearls of dew form, clear and bright.   5
At dawn, the snowy mountain's hermit
gathers the rare tea's early leaves
where rising mist shrouds rocky rapids,
hardly a foot below the red cliff's ledge.
Round or square, his fine, lacquered boxes
hold tea like flawless court jade.
I call my servant to light the bronze stove.
The lingering scent reaches distant retreats.
Purifying thoughts, it reveals one's true self,
returning to the source to clear foul and evil.
It's like Buddha's holy meal, sweet dew,
with a scent that fills the whole of Vaiśālī.[4]
O! These companions from the immortals' islands—[5]
aren't they worth more than Rose-Light Wine?[6]

芙蓉亭

新亭俯朱槛
嘉木开芙蓉
清香晨风远
溽彩寒露浓
潇洒出人世
低昂多异容
尝闻色空喻
造物谁为工
留连秋月晏
迢递来山钟

Cotton Rose Pavilion[7]

The new pavilion overlooks a red railing.
Fine cotton roses unfurl their blossoms.
Their pure scent travels far on the dawn breeze
while pearls of cold dew sharpen their damp colors.
Free, at ease, they transcend this mortal world,
lifting and drooping in countless lovely poses.
I've heard the teaching on the emptiness of forms;[8]
as for everything's creation: who's the craftsman?
I linger in the clear autumn moonlight.
The temple bell drifts from far-off mountains.

苦竹桥

危桥属幽径
缭绕穿疏林
迸箨分苦节
轻筠抱虚心
俯瞰涓涓流
仰聆萧萧吟
差池下烟日
嘲哳鸣山禽
谅无要津用
栖息有余阴

Bitter Bamboo Bridge[9]

A high bridge connects a quiet path
that twists and coils as it pierces a sparse grove.
Growing sheaths split to reveal fresh, bitter nodes,
and limber rinds enclose open hearts.[10]
Looking down, I glimpse a murmuring stream.
Looking up, I hear whispered chants.
The last sunrays turn ragged in the haze
and mountain birds make a racket.
This bamboo might be unfit for major fords[11]
but its shade is good enough to rest in.

江雪

千山鸟飞绝
万径人踪灭
孤舟蓑笠翁
独钓寒江雪

River Snow[12]

No bird hovers above a thousand hills.
No footprint remains on ten thousand trails.
One boat: an old man in a straw raincoat
is fishing alone in cold river snow.

红蕉

晚英值穷节
绿润含朱光
以兹正阳色
窈窕凌清霜
远物世所重
旅人心独伤
回晖眺林际
槭槭无遗芳

Scarlet Canna[13]

Its late bloom faces the season's end,
a scarlet sheen cradled in its green gloss,
so that now, in early summer's tones,
fair and graceful, it overcomes the cold frost.
These days people value far-off things
while the exile's heart aches alone.
The last sunlight sweeps across the woods.
A whispered patter: no blossom stays.

早梅

早梅发高树
迥映楚天碧
朔吹飘夜香
繁霜滋晓白
欲为万里赠
杳杳山水隔
寒英坐销落
何用慰远客

Early Plum[14]

The tall tree sends out early plum blossoms
set against the distant Chu sky's blue.
A north wind spreads their nighttime fragrance
and heavy frost powders their faces at dawn.
I'd give them to the one who's ten thousand miles away
but endless mountains and waters intervene.
Cold blossoms wilt and fall so quickly,
how can they comfort a wanderer far from home?

梅雨

梅实迎时雨
苍茫值晚春
愁深楚猿夜
梦断越鸡晨
海雾连南极
江云暗北津
素衣今尽化
非为帝京尘

Plum Rains[15]

Plum fruits welcome the season's rains.
A heavy mist veils the waning spring.
Sorrows deepen: Chu gibbons cry at night.
Dreams cut short: a Yue rooster crows at dawn.[16]
Fog and water merge to the farthest south
while river clouds darken the north fords.
My white gown is filthy now
but not because of the capital's dust.

17

南中荣橘柚

橘柚怀贞质
受命此炎方
密林耀朱绿
晚岁有余芳
殊风限清汉
飞雪滞故乡
攀条何所叹
北望熊与湘

Prospering Tangerine Trees in the South[17]

Tangerine's virtue is its firm devotion
to fate, which placed it here in the hot south.[18]
In dense woods it shines red and green
and its scent lingers late into the year.
The Huai River separates north and south.[19]
Whirling snow shrouds my homeland.
Pulling down a branch, why do I sigh?
I'm looking north for Mounts Xiong and Xiang.[20]

戏题阶前芍药

凡卉与时谢
妍华丽兹晨
欹红醉浓露
窈窕留余春
孤赏白日暮
暄风动摇频
夜窗蔼芳气
幽卧知相亲
愿致溱洧赠
悠悠南国人

20

A Playful Poem on a Garden Peony

Fronting the Steps[21]

While common plants decline with the season,
one radiant blossom is stunning this dawn:
tipsy, crimson, drunk with heavy dew,
its elegance lingers in the last of the spring.
It admires itself until daylight's end
as a warm breeze stirs it again and again.
At night, its sweet breath fills my window.
Lying in darkness, I feel it draw near.
How I wish I could, like the youths at Zhen and Wei,[22]
present it to a graceful southern maiden!

湘岸移木芙蓉植龙兴精舍

有美不自蔽
安能守孤根
盈盈湘西岸
秋至风露繁
丽影别寒水
秾芳委前轩
芰荷谅难杂
反此生高原

On Transplanting a Cotton Rose
from the Xiang River's Shore
to Longxing Temple House[23]

Radiant, and not demure about it,
how could it stay rooted alone?
Graceful, it stood on the Xiang River's west bank.
Autumn arrived, wind and dew gathering.
Its striking reflection left the cold water
to offer its rich scent at my veranda.
Life must have been hard down there among lotus,
so instead it settled here on high ground.

23

自衡阳移桂十余本植零陵所住精舍

谪官去南裔
清湘绕灵岳
晨登蒹葭岸
霜景霁纷浊
离披得幽桂
芳本欣盈握
火耕困烟烬
薪采久摧剥
道旁且不愿
岑岭况悠邈
倾筐壅故壤
栖息期鸾鷟
路远清凉宫
一雨悟无学
南人始珍重
微我谁先觉
芳意不可传
丹心徒自渥

On Transplanting Ten-Odd Sweet Osmanthus Trees from Hengyang to the Temple House Where I Live in Lingling[24]

Demoted, sent to the southern border
where the clear Xiang River skirts Heng Mountain,
at dawn I climb its reed-lined bank,
seeing frost, a sky cleared of dust and mist.
In a dense grove, I find secluded osmanthus trees
and rejoice, clasping their scented trunks.
They've nearly choked in slash-and-burn farming's smoke
and years of wood gathering have flayed them.
People don't even care for roadside plants,
so what of those in remote, rugged mountains?
I transplant them with a basket of their old soil,
hoping someday phoenixes will perch there.
While their elder thrives at the far-off moon's palace,
a single rain enlightens them.[25]
Few Southerners used to value these trees.
Without me, who would know their significance?
Their scent's meaning can't be conveyed
so they stand alone, purehearted.

种白蘘荷

皿虫化为疠
夷俗多所神
衔猜每腊毒
谋富不为仁
蔬果自远至
杯酒盈肆陈
言甘中必苦
何用知其真
华洁事外饰
尤病中州人
钱刀恐贾害
饥至益逡巡
窜伏常战栗
怀故逾悲辛
庶氏有嘉草
攻襘事久泯
炎帝垂灵编
言此殊足珍
崎岖乃有得
托以全余身
纷敷碧树阴
眄睐心所亲

Planting White Myoga Ginger[26]

Of a pot of insects, the most toxic survives.[27]
Barbarian customs treat it as a spirit
but I suspect drinks made with it tend to be deadly
and the greedy ones who sell them are unkind.
Fruits and vegetables arrive from far off.
Cups of wine fill the market stalls.
The core of sweet speech is often bitter—
how can I know if it's true or false?
The neat and gaudy serve as mere gilding
for those who aim to sicken this Northerner.
I'm afraid money will buy only harm,
but the hungrier I am, the more I cower.
In exile here, I often shiver and shudder.
Thinking of home, my grief sharpens further.
Faith healing as a cure has long been lost
but Shushi left us a remedy with this Fine Herb[28]
and Yandi[29] passed down the sacred work
that tells us it's especially precious.
You only find it on rough and rugged land.
I rely on it for my well-being.
It thrives in an emerald tree's shade.
Now and then, I glance at my heart's companion.

种仙灵毗

穷陌阙自养
疠气剧嚣烦
隆冬乏霜霰
日夕南风温
杖藜下庭际
曳踵不及门
门有野田吏
慰我飘零魂
及言有灵药
近在湘西原
服之不盈旬
鳌蹇皆腾骞
笑抃前即吏
为我擢其根
蔚蔚遂充庭
英翘忽已繁
晨起自采曝
杵臼通夜喧
灵和理内藏
攻疾贵自源
壅覆逃积雾
伸舒委余暄
奇功苟可征
宁复资兰荪
我闻畸人术
一气中夜存

Planting Fairy Wings[30]

In this poor, shabby place, I barely keep well
as the toxic air troubles me to no end.
Midwinter here lacks hail or frost;
every evening, the south wind's lukewarm.
Cane in hand, I descend to the courtyard's edge
but my heels drag and I can hardly reach my gate.
At the gate is the Official of Cleared Lands
who comforts my drifting, withered spirit
when he tells me about a magic herb
nearby, in a field west of the Xiang River:
"Take the herb for no more than ten days
and your limps will become leaps and soars."
I smile, clap, and hurry toward the official,
begging him to pull the plant at its roots for me.
Dense and lush, it soon fills my courtyard
with clusters of sudden, bright blossoms.
At dawn, I rise to pick and sun-dry them.
My pestle and mortar sound all through the night.
These mild fairy wings balance my insides—
the best place to treat an illness is at its source.
They scatter and oust my feverish mists
then, stretching, they cast off excess warmth.
If only I could prove this magic feat,
I wouldn't need to keep buying sweet sedge.
I've heard of certain odd people's skills,
how they can hold one breath half the night.

能令深深息
呼吸还归跟
疏放固难效
且以药饵论
痿者不忘起
穷者宁复言
神哉辅吾足
幸及儿女奔

It requires them to breathe very deeply
while feeling the air flow up from their soles.
Self-indulgent, I'd have trouble with that,
so I'll keep taking medicine instead.
Those who are paralyzed don't forget to get up
and those who are poor say, "I must rise again,"
so come on, magic herb, help my feet,
make me lucky enough to run like a child!

植灵寿木

白华鉴寒水
怡我适野情
前趋问长老
重复欣嘉名
蹇连易衰朽
方刚谢经营
敢期齿杖赐
聊且移孤茎
丛萼中竞秀
分房外舒英
柔条乍反植
劲节常对生
循玩足忘疲
稍觉步武轻
安能事翦伐
持用资徒行

Planting the Tree of Longevity[31]

Cold water mirrors its white blossoms,
satisfying my desire for wilderness.
I hurry to ask the elder about it
and rejoice again over its fine name.
Suffering hard times, I've decayed quickly
and lost all ambition, though still in my prime.
How could I hope for the honor of an Elder's Cane?[32]
Tentatively, I transplant this lone sapling.
Amid clustered blossoms, it strives to show its beauty,
unfurling its petals in front of my side rooms.
Its pliant branches grow straight down
and its strong knots often appear in pairs.
Stroking it is enough to forget my fatigue
as, faintly, I feel a spring in my step.
How could I possibly cut it down
and use it to lean on while walking?

種朮

守闲事服饵
采朮东山阿
东山幽且阻
疲苶烦经过
戒徒斸灵根
封植阆天和
违尔涧底石
彻我庭中莎
土膏滋玄液
松露坠繁柯
南东自成亩
缭绕纷相罗
晨步佳色媚
夜眠幽气多
离忧苟可怡
孰能知其他
爨竹茹芳叶
宁虑瘵与瘥
留连树蕙辝
婉娈采薇歌
悟拙甘自足
激清愧同波
单豹且理内
高门复如何

Planting Bai Zhu[33]

To kill time, I busy myself with medicine,
searching for *bai zhu* on the East Mountains' slopes.
The East Mountains are dark; their paths are impassable.
Tired and weak, I have trouble walking them.
I tell my servant to hoe the magic root,
plant it and pile earth to store heaven's harmony.
So you take leave of the rocky ravine
while I clear the nutgrass from my yard.
Murky water wets *bai zhu*'s rich soil
and pine dew falls on its dense foliage.
This herb abounds in all directions,
thriving twigs and leaves interlacing.
On morning walks, its beauty charms me.
At night, when I sleep, its secret scent strengthens.
If only it could cure my exile's worries,
what else would I possibly need?
Once I've eaten its sweet leaves boiled over bamboo,
why should I worry about pain and disease?
I linger on those lines about planting boat orchids[34]
and the tender song, "Gathering *Osmunda* Ferns."
Recognizing my folly, I'm content now
but, recalling our reforms, I'm ashamed to face my comrades.[35]
For now, like Shan Bao, I focus on my health.
As for those living behind lofty gates—who cares?[36]

秋晓行南谷经荒村

杪秋霜露重
晨起行幽谷
黄叶覆溪桥
荒村唯古木
寒花疏寂历
幽泉微断续
机心久已忘
何事惊麋鹿

Autumn Dawn, Visiting South Valley and Passing through an Abandoned Village[37]

Autumn's edge. Frosty dew is heavy.
Dawn, I rise and visit a quiet valley.
Yellow leaves blanket a creek bridge.
An abandoned village: only old trees.
Cold blossoms all sparse and silent.
A solitary spring, thin and intermittent.
I've long given up on scheming,
so why does the elk start from me?

夏初雨后寻愚溪

悠悠雨初霁
独绕清溪曲
引杖试荒泉
解带围新竹
沉吟亦何事
寂寞固所欲
幸此息营营
啸歌静炎燠

After an Early Summer Rain,
Exploring Foolish Creek[38]

As soon as the long rain has ended,
I trace Foolish Creek's bends alone,
using my cane to gauge wild springs,
untying my sash belt to corral young bamboo.
So why do I still drift and waver?
I've wanted this solitude a long time.
Feeling lucky I've left the social ladder,
I chant to quiet the blistering heat.

冉溪

少时陈力希公侯
许国不复为身谋
风波一跌逝万里
壮心瓦解空缧囚
缧囚终老无余事
愿卜湘西冉溪地.
却学寿张樊敬侯
种漆南园待成器

40

Ran Creek

Showing talent from early on, I longed to be a marquis[39]
and devoted myself to my country without selfish aims;
but one wave of trouble has tossed me ten thousand miles,
my ambition crumbled to pieces—an unbound prisoner—
a prisoner, with nothing to do for the rest of my days.
Just let me choose a place on Ran Creek, west of the Xiang River.
There, I'll learn from Fan Jing, the Marquis of Shouzhang,
who planted lacquer in his south garden for later use.[40]

溪居

久为簪组累
幸此南夷谪
闲依农圃邻
偶似山林客
晓耕翻露草
夜榜响溪石
来往不逢人
长歌楚天碧

Creekside Living[41]

Long burdened by my official headwear,
I'm lucky, demoted to the southern border.
Idle, I lounge among farms and orchards.
Other times, I resemble a mountain recluse.
At dawn I plow and turn the dewy sod.
At night my oar echoes off creek rocks.
Coming and going, encountering no one,
I sing on and on to the blue Chu sky.

茅檐下始栽竹

瘴茅葺为宇
溽暑常侵肌
适有重膇疾
蒸郁宁所宜
东邻幸导我
树竹邀凉飔
欣然惬吾志
荷锸西岩垂
楚壤多怪石
垦凿力已疲
江风忽云暮
舆曳还相追
萧瑟过极浦
旖旎附幽墀
贞根期永固
贻尔寒泉滋
夜窗遂不掩
羽扇宁复持
清泠集浓露
枕簟凄已知
网虫依密叶
晓禽栖迥枝
岂伊纷嚣间
重以心虑怡

Starting to Plant Bamboo
under My Thatched Eaves[42]

My house is thatched with foul-air grass.
The muggy heat assaults my body.
Even my feet swell and ache.
How can I bear this steamy house?
Luckily, my east neighbor advised me
to plant bamboo to entice the cool breeze.
This nicely aligns with my desires
so I carry my shovel to the west cliff.
Many strange stones in the Chu soil
exhaust me as I struggle to dig there.
A river breeze—clouds bring sudden dusk.
I chase after my bamboo-loaded cart.[43]
Bamboo leaves rustle as I cross the remote river.
Tender and graceful, they adorn my secluded steps.
I plant them straight, hoping they'll always stand firm,
and nurture them with cold spring water.
Now I no longer close the window at night
and no longer hold a feather fan
since the bamboo gather glistening, cold dew
and my bamboo pillow already feels cool.
Spiders cling to their dense foliage.
Morning birds perch on their outer twigs.
How, amid the world's hustle and bustle,
have I managed to calm my heart's cares!

嘉尔亭亭质
自远弃幽期
不见野蔓草
蓊蔚有华姿
谅无凌寒色
岂与青山辞

I admire their slender uprightness.
They've traveled far, abandoning former loves.
Who hasn't seen the wild creeping grass
that is so garish, lush, and lovely?
But, helpless to resist the cold,
could it ever leave the green mountains?

新植海石榴

弱植不盈尺
远意驻蓬瀛
月寒空阶曙
幽梦彩云生
粪壤擢珠树
莓苔插琼英
芳根闷颜色
徂岁为谁荣

Newly Planted Camellia[44]

This frail seedling hasn't reached a foot,
though it longs to grow back on the immortals' islands.[45]
The moon's cold, the empty stairs wait for dawn
while, in its quiet dreams, splendid clouds appear.
From rich manure, this pearl tree has sprouted.
Out of moss, its jasper blossoms will emerge.
For now, it hides its bright spirit in its roots,
but in years past, for whom has it bloomed?

49

渔翁

渔翁夜傍西岩宿
晓汲清湘燃楚竹
烟销日出不见人
欸乃一声山水绿
回看天际下中流
岩上无心云相逐

50

Old Fisherman[46]

An old fisherman moors at dusk by the west cliffs.
At dawn, he burns Chu bamboo to boil the Xiang's clear water.
The smoke melts in the sunrise, but he's nowhere in sight.
One oar's splash—green mountains and waters sharpen.
Midway downriver now, he looks back at the horizon.
Above the cliffs, aimless clouds chase one another.

51

始见白发题所植海石榴树

几年封植爱芳丛
韶艳朱颜竟不同
从此休论上春事
看成古木对衰翁

Starting to See White Hair:
On the Camellia I Planted[47]

Through year after year of nurture, I've loved this sweet shrub.
Today, my cheeks no longer share its radiant blush.
From now on let's not mention any spring sowing—
only an old tree face-to-face with a withered old man.

53

入黄溪闻猿

溪路千里曲
哀猿何处鸣
孤臣泪已尽
虚作断肠声

54

Entering Yellow Creek,
Hearing the Gibbons

The creek path meanders for a thousand miles.
From where come the mournful gibbons' cries?
This lone official's tears have dried up.
Their heartbroken wails are pointless now.[48]

55

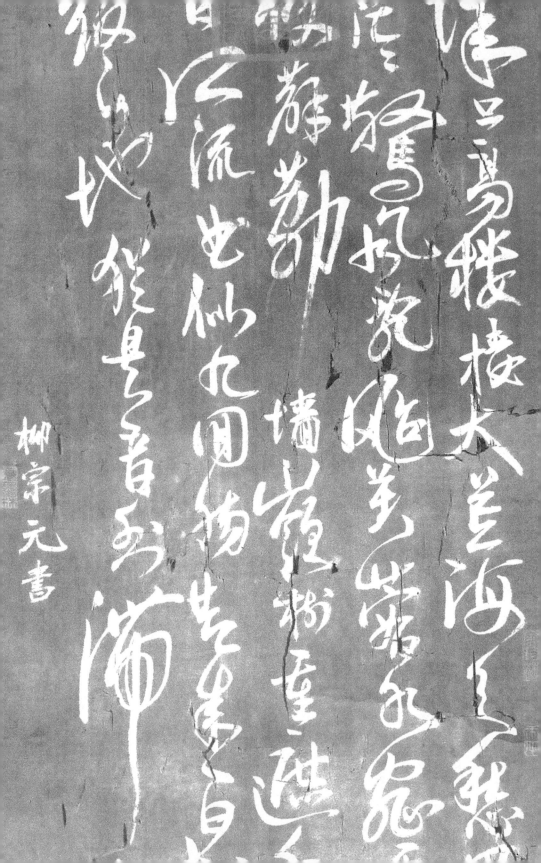

柳宗元書

Interlude (815)

IN 815, EMPEROR XIANZONG UNEXPECTEDLY ENDED Liu Zongyuan's exile in Yongzhou, and Liu returned to Chang'an. Delighted, Liu rekindled his fading political ambition. But, after a brief one-month stay in the capital, Liu was exiled even farther away to Liuzhou. In this transitional section, the first poem, composed on Liu's return to the capital, implies his secret hope that the emperor would recognize his talent. In the second poem, written on Liu's journey from Chang'an to Liuzhou, Liu complains about the jealousy and slander of his political enemies, his gratitude toward his friends for their help, as well as his flickering (but never extinguished) hope for the emperor's favor.

清水驿丛竹天水赵云余手种一十二茎

檐下疏篁十二茎
襄阳从事寄幽情
祇应更使伶伦见
写尽雌雄双凤鸣

Mr. Zhao from Tianshui Plants
Twelve Bamboo by Hand at
Clear Water Courier Station

Below the eaves, twelve bamboo stems have been scattered
to convey the Xianyang official's deep feelings.
Now that they're here, he might well send for Ling Lun,
who'd compose all the phoenix couple's songs.[49]

商山临路有孤松往来斫以为明好事
者怜之编竹成援遂其生植感而赋诗

60

孤松停翠盖
托根临广路
不以险自防
遂为明所误
幸逢仁惠意
重此藩篱护
犹有半心存
时将承雨露

Overlooking the Road on Shang Mountain
Is a Lone Pine. Coming and Going,
People Cut Its Branches to Make Torches
until a Benefactor Protected It with
a Bamboo Fence to Help It Grow.
Moved by This, I Compose a Poem. [50]

61

Alone, the tall pine with its emerald canopy
roots here, overlooking a wide road.
It didn't protect itself with a narrow pass
so, sought for torches, it came to harm.
Fortunately, it fell into merciful hands
that saw its true worth and fenced it in.
Now, with half its heart still unscathed,
it's ready for the rain's blessing from on high.

PART TWO: *Liuzhou* (815–819)

I N THE SUMMER OF 815, LIU ZONGYUAN ARRIVED in Liuzhou. Liu's early days in his new home paralleled those in Yongzhou in a few ways. One of the two family members who joined him in Liuzhou, a thirty-two-year-old cousin, died a month after their arrival. Liu quickly fell ill again, this time with ulcers and cholera. Ailments, including bloating, palpitations, and the thiamine deficiency he had contracted in Yongzhou, would contribute to his death four years later. As in Yongzhou, he was intensely aware of the social, political, and cultural marginality of his life in exile.

However, for the most part, Liu's life in Liuzhou was very different from what it had been in Yongzhou. As a prefect, Liu finally had the authority to implement his political ideas at a local level. His responsibilities encompassed many aspects of life in Liuzhou. His most renowned, and perhaps most significant, act was ending the widespread practice that involved parents using their children as loan collateral. When parents were unable to repay their loans, they would be compelled to hand their children over to their creditors. Liu passed a law demanding that creditors give child slaves back pay equivalent to servants' wages as compensation for the children's time in servitude. When the wages were sufficient to repay the debt, the child was released from bondage. Liu also apparently contributed some of his own wealth to releasing child slaves in the area. Other Tang officials took note of his policy and applied it elsewhere in the empire.[51]

Liu wrote much less in Liuzhou than he had in Yongzhou. Many of his Liuzhou compositions are occasional pieces: letters, ceremonial inscriptions, poems on memorable events, and the like. He kept up his passion for gardening in Liuzhou, however, and one of his favorite inspirations for an occasional poem seems to have been planting a new plant. As a prefect, Liu could also scale up his gardening projects. While most poems in Yongzhou describe planting one or a few plants, Liu opens "In Liuzhou's Northwest Corner, Planting Mandarin Trees" [《柳州城西北隅种甘树》] with the line, "We've planted two hundred mandarin trees by hand." Eventually, as Liu's friend Han Yu writes, the area came to resemble something like an enormous garden: "The city became tidy and streets were lined with pretty trees, people had new homes and boats, clean ponds and yards, fat fowl and livestock."[52] In 819, surrounded by his new cultivated landscape, Liu finally succumbed to disease. Around the same time, Prime Minister Pei Du [裴度] (765–839) managed to persuade Emperor Xianzong to recall Liu to Chang'an. But the imperial decree failed to reach Liu before his death.[53]

酬贾鹏山人郡内新栽松寓兴见赠二首

一

芳朽自为别
无心乃玄功
夭夭日放花
荣耀将安穷
青松遗涧底
擢莳兹庭中
积雪表明秀
寒花助葱茏
幽贞夙有慕
持以延清风

*For Hermit Jia Peng: On Transplanting
a New Pine in the Prefecture to
Convey Feelings (Two Poems)*[54]

I.

Fragrant and rotten are naturally distinct;
a pure heart is the work of heaven.
Flourishing blossoms unfurl in the sun,
but how soon will their radiance end?
A green pine, left at the ravine's base,
has been transplanted to this courtyard.
Deep snow highlights its bright beauty
and winter blossoms sharpen its dense greens.
Long admired, secluded and chaste,
it invites the fresh breeze for us.

67

酬贾鹏山人郡内新栽松寓兴见赠二首

二

68

无能常闭阁
偶以静见名
奇姿来远山
忽似人家生
劲色不改旧
芳心与谁荣
喧卑岂所安
任物非我情
清韵动筝瑟
谐此风中声

For Hermit Jia Peng: On Transplanting
a New Pine in the Prefecture to
Convey Feelings (Two Poems)

II.

A good-for-nothing, I tend to keep my door shut,
so people call me a quiet person.

A rare sight, this pine arrived from distant mountains
but it grows as if born in this courtyard.
Its strong character hasn't changed since ancient times.
For whom does its fragrant heart flourish?
How could one settle among the strident and vulgar?
Casualness isn't in my nature.
The zither and reed organ stir—a clear melody
harmonizes with the wind singing through it.

柳州二月榕叶落尽偶题

宦情羁思共凄凄
春半如秋意转迷
山城过雨百花尽
榕叶满庭莺乱啼

In Liuzhou, Second Month, the Banyan Leaves Have All Fallen: An Occasional Poem[55]

Demoted, exiled—my thoughts and feelings all sting
and my mind's dazed by this mid-spring that seems like autumn.
Rain whips through this mountain city. Countless blossoms fall.
Banyan leaves fill the courtyard, and the orioles riot.

种柳戏题

柳州柳刺史
种柳柳江边
谈笑为故事
推移成昔年
垂阴当覆地
耸干会参天
好作思人树
惭无惠化传

A Playful Poem on Planting Willows[56]

I, Willow Prefecture's prefect——Mr. Willow——[57]
plant a willow along the Willow River.
People will smile and chat about this old tale
when the year's become ancient history.
Its drooping shelter will shade the ground
and its upright trunk will touch the sky.
It will serve as my "memorial tree,"[58]
though I'm ashamed I haven't achieved much.

柳州城西北隅种甘树

手种黄甘二百株
春来新叶徧城隅
方同楚客怜皇树
不学荆州利木奴
几岁开花闻喷雪
何人摘实见垂珠
若教坐待成林日
滋味还堪养老夫

In Liuzhou's Northwest Corner, Planting Mandarin Trees[59]

We've planted two hundred mandarin trees by hand.
Now, when spring arrives, new leaves thrive in this corner of town.
Like Qu Yuan of Chu, I adore these "glorious trees"
and won't enslave them for gain like that Jingzhou man.[60]
How many years before one smells their snowy blossoms?
When their fruits hang like pearls, who will see and pluck them?
If I have to wait here while they grow into a grove,
at least their nectar will sustain me when I'm old.

种木槲花

上苑年年占物华
飘零今日在天涯
祇应长作龙城守
剩种庭前木槲花

Planting Noble Dendrobium[61]

Each year, the Imperial Park fills with the finest blossoms,
but today, at the world's end, I'm withered and adrift.
As Liuzhou's warden, I'll have to stay here a long time.
All I can do is plant noble dendrobium in my yard.

1. From Han Yu's "The Epigraph for Liu Zihou" [《柳子厚墓志铭》] in *Collected Works of Liu Hedong* [《柳河东文集》], 847.

2. Liu composed this poem on Buddhism and tea in 806. Master Chong Xun [重巽], the head of Longxing Temple, invited Liu to have tea picked by the master himself. Liu describes several aspects of the tea's excellence. First, the tea plants grow in a particularly favorable location: among Xiang bamboo near water flowing below the peak of a mist-shrouded mountain. Such a location is so beautiful and secluded that Liu compares it to the legendary islands where immortals were said to reside. Second, Master Chong Xun picked the tea at the best time: in the early morning, when dew sits heavy on the leaves. Third, he picked the prime tea leaves—furled young leaves, which are like flawless court jade. Last, the tea is contained in the best tea boxes, round or square in gorgeous colors. Therefore, the tea is of the highest quality, rare and precious. Liu compares the tea to a mythical immortal's Rose-Light Wine. Similar to these other legendary drinks, Liu's tea has a fragrance and taste that reach far, purifying body and soul. Chong Xun, who, like many other reverent monks, chose to lead a reclusive ascetic life in the mountains, encapsulates the relationship between tea and spirituality.

3. Also called Xiangfei bamboo or bamboo with Xiang Concubine's Tears, this is a type of bamboo with tear-like speckles on its stems that usually grows in Hunan Province, the short name of which is Xiang.

4. Buddha's holy meal, sweet dew, is reported once to have filled the entire ancient Indian city of Vaiśālī.

5. Peng and Ying are legendary islands where immortals were believed to live.

6. Supposedly brewed by an immortal, Rose-Light Wine is said to look like flowing rose-tinted sunlight.

7. This poem and the next are two of the five poems about various scenic locations in Longxing Temple [《巽公院五咏》] composed in 806. Cotton rose (*Hibiscus mutabilis*) is a plant in the mallow family (*Malvaceae*) native to South China. It can take the form of a shrub or tree, often reaching between roughly five and fifteen feet tall. It has broad, green, lobed leaves and large blossoms that somewhat resemble those in the rose family (*Rosaceae*). The plant has long been admired in China, where it symbolizes beauty. For instance, in the eighteenth-century novel *Dream of the Red Chamber* [《红楼梦》], the character Qing Wen is believed to transform into the "Goddess of the Cotton Rose" after her death.

8. The blossoms of some cotton roses change color over time—shifting from white to pink, then red—which might have reminded Liu Zongyuan of the Buddhist doctrine on the emptiness of forms (i.e., the realization that worldly forms are ultimately empty and to be transcended).

9. Bitter bamboo (*Pleioblastuc amarus* [*Keng*]) is a bamboo species native to South China that reaches roughly three to fifteen feet tall.

10. In these two lines, Liu uses puns to extol two virtues often metaphorically represented by the bamboo in China: 「苦节」 evokes both "bitter nodes" and "strict temperance," which are homophones, while 「虚心」 refers to both the bamboo's empty core and an untroubled, humble heart.

11. In Chinese literature, "major fords" is a common metaphor for important positions in society. In contrast to bamboo species such as *mao zhu* (*Phyllostachys edulis*) [毛竹], which has sturdy stems that reach more than sixty feet tall, bitter bamboo is somewhat short and weak. For this reason, it is also literally unfit to build "major fords."

12. "River Snow," composed in 807, is Liu's most anthologized poem.

13. Liu composed this poem in 808. The piece seems to refer to a species in the *Canna* genus. These plants are herbaceous perennials that somewhat resemble lilies and are related to gingers (order Zingiberales). While they are native to the Americas, they were cultivated in South China as early as the Tang Dynasty. At the time, only individuals with scarlet blossoms were found in the country, so the plant was called "scarlet canna." It was considered rare by northerners. These days, canna with blossoms in a range of colors can be found in China and elsewhere around the world.

14. Liu composed this poem in Yongzhou, but exactly when is unclear. Chinese plum (*Prunus mume*) is one of the two national flowers of China, the other being peony. It blooms early in the year, often when snow and frost are still present, and is seen as an auspicious herald of spring. The tree's form is considered elegant, and the image of blooming branches bent under the weight of snow or frost frequently represents gracefulness enduring under pressure. The tree appears widely in Chinese literature and painting.

15. Liu composed this poem in 809. In the mid-low reaches of the Yangzi River, there is an annual monsoon season at the time Chinese plums ripen (usually lasting about a month in late spring or early summer). Therefore, this time of year is called the Plum Rain Season. As the saying goes, "When the rain starts to hit yellow plums, you will see no sun for forty-five days." The season is particularly difficult for exiles from the north, where the climate is much drier. The experience of this season was often represented in Chinese literature. See, for example, Du Fu's poem with the same title and Su Shi's poems on the topic. (Our thanks to Prof. Paula Varsano for the references to Du Fu and Su Shi.)

16. Yongzhou sits in the south of the ancient Chu Kingdom and the north of the ancient Yue Kingdom.

17. Liu composed this poem in Yongzhou, but exactly when is unclear. The title is a quote from "A Poem in Reward for the Kindness of Wang Deyuan from Jin'an" [《酬王晋安德元诗》] by Xie Tiao) [谢朓] (464–499). The plant [橘柚] clearly refers to citrus trees, though the exact species is uncertain. It is likely a variety of *Citrus reticulata*, such as the tangerine. This species is different from

the one described in "Planting Two Hundred Mandarin Trees by Hand" [甘树], though both seem to be varieties of *Citrus reticulata*.

18. The first two lines allude to Qu Yuan's [屈原] (340–278 BCE) comment in "Ode to Tangerine" [《橘颂》]: "The beautiful tangerine tree is predestined to live in the south. It is hard to transplant with its unshakable loyalty." It is said that the tangerine tree bears fruits large and sweet in the south, but the fruits grow small and bitter in the north. In contrast with the tangerine tree's loyalty to the south, Liu Zongyuan implies his allegiance to the north, where his hometown and the capital are located. Qu Yuan was the greatest poet of the Kingdom of Chu. Once a high-ranking official, Qu Yuan was banished by the emperor and eventually committed suicide. In his poetry, Qu Yuan regularly uses plants to signify various people and attributes. Liu Zongyuan admired and often compared himself to Qu Yuan, especially after Liu's demotion.

19. [清汉] usually means the Milky Way but here, by extension, it refers to the Huai River [淮河], the traditional division between North and South China. Liu's position south of the river, gazing north, emphasizes his homesickness.

20. Mount Xiong, or Mount Xiong'er, is in modern Henan Province; Mount Xiang is in modern Hubei Province. The two mountains are both far north of Yongzhou.

21. Liu probably composed this poem in 809. Garden peony (*Paeonia lactiflora*), also called Chinese peony, is a shrub-like perennial native to North China. A late-blooming species, it produces three-to-six-inch white, pink, or crimson, cup-shaped blossoms, and is renowned for its strong, lovely fragrance.

22. According to the *Shijing* or *Book of Songs* [《诗经》], in ancient times young men and young women played together and exchanged peonies (generally expressing love) along the Zhen River and the Wei River in spring. Liu's first wife died in 799. This poem seems to imply his intention to find a partner in the area. He later had a concubine in Yongzhou, who gave birth to his second daughter in 810. The earliest poetic anthology in China, the *Shijing* comprises 311 poems ranging from the eleventh to sixth centuries BCE.

23. It's unclear when Liu composed this poem, but it must have been before he moved out of Longxing Temple in 809. See "Cotton Rose Pavilion" for more information on cotton rose (*Hibiscus mutabilis*).

24. It's unclear when Liu composed this poem, but, like "On Transplanting a Cotton Rose from the Xiang River's Shore to Longxing Temple," it must have been before he moved out of Longxing Temple in 809. Sweet osmanthus (*Osmanthus fragrans*) is an evergreen shrub or tree native to South China and elsewhere in Asia. Reaching roughly ten to forty feet tall, it has green leaves and produces small, highly fragrant, white, yellow, or coral flowers between autumn and spring. It has long held a prominent place in Chinese culture.

25. According to ancient Chinese folklore, Chang E [嫦娥], a beautiful goddess, lives in the Cold Palace on the moon, in front of which grows a huge sweet osmanthus tree. The Chinese idiom "picking an osmanthus branch at the Cold Palace" [蟾宫折桂] means earning the highest place in *keju* exams or other national exams.

Here, the concept of "enlightenment" relates to the Buddhist concept of *Asekha* (the highest state of realization, at which point one needs no further learning).

26. It's thought Liu composed this poem between 809 and 810. After being cheated by a druggist in 809, Liu decided to plant herbs himself. See this book's introduction for more details on white myoga ginger (*Zingiber mioga*).

27. This line refers to a supposed practice among the peoples of South China that appears in several literary works on the region. For example, the *History of the Sui Dynasty: Geography Annals* (*Suishu dili zhi*) [《隋书地理志》] (compiled 636 CE) reads:

> Thus these numerous regions (Poyang [鄱阳] and Jiujiang [九江] counties in modern Jiangxi Province [江西], and various other regions) often store up the *gu* [蛊] insect, and Yichun city [宜春] (in Jiangxi Province) deviates to the extreme. In their method, they use the fifth day of the fifth month to gather one hundred kinds of lower animal life (e.g., insects, larvae, worms), the biggest being a serpent, the smallest being a louse. They are placed together in a vessel and made to eat each other. When one type remains, they preserve it, and whether a snake or a louse is that day's *gu*, it is effective for killing a person. The reason is that, eating, it enters a person's stomach, feeding on his five viscera until he dies. Then, on its giving birth, it moves to enter the *gu* owner's house. For three years it doesn't kill another person, then the one who raised it himself concentrates its evil. Accumulated generations of offspring have passed this down without abjuring it, and we also have it according to a woman who married there. Gan Bao [干宝] (d. 336) calls them demons, but in fact this is not so.

While this process involved animals such as snakes and worms, the majority of animals were insects, and the result was always called the "*gu* insect."

28. Shushi is the title of an ancient minor official whose duty was to treat poisoning. "Fine Herb" is another name for white myoga ginger.

29. Yandi [炎帝], also known as the Flame Emperor or Shennong, was a legendary early Chinese ruler who was thought to have taught agriculture and the use of herbal medicines to the ancient Chinese people.

30. Liu might have composed this poem in 809 or 810. Fairy wings (*Epimedium* sp.) (the character [仙] in its name means "fairy" or "immortal"), also known as "horny goat weed," refers to a genus of rhizomatous perennials in the barberry family (*Berberidaceae*). Most species are native to China, where the plant has a long history of medicinal use. In traditional Chinese medicine, doctors often prescribe recipes containing multiple ingredients. Fairy wings is included in recipes to strengthen bones and muscles, increase energy, and resolve erectile dysfunction, among other uses.

31. Liu composed this poem in 809. Suffering from swollen feet caused by thiamine deficiency, Liu needed a walking stick. In ancient China, it was said that the tree of longevity provided the best walking stick material. See the introduction and note 32 below for more information on the tree of longevity.

32. The Elder's Cane is also called the Senior-Respecting Cane [敬老杖], the Imperial Cane [王杖], or the Turtledove Cane [鸠杖], among other titles. The stems of the tree of longevity are light and tough, with node rings similar to those of bamboo and a good width for gripping, so there's no need to trim them when they're made into canes. Since ancient times, Chinese people have believed these stems are the best material for elders' walking canes. Therefore, the tree was named the tree of longevity, and the area where many trees of longevity were discovered was founded as Longevity County in the Han Dynasty in 204 BCE. The head of the cane was usually carved in the shape of a turtledove (which is believed never to choke) as a good omen for the elderly, hence the name Turtledove Cane. According to the "Imperial Edict Concerning the Imperial Canes" [《王杖诏书令》] enacted at the beginning of the Han Dynasty, the central government would confer a turtledove-headed cane on those over seventy years old. The elders with such a cane had many privileges, such as an exemption from taxation, work duty, and penalties for misdemeanors, as well as the privilege of walking beside the emperor's bridleway. The people who offended cane-holding elders would be punished severely, sometimes even with death. According to "Kong Guang's Biography" in the *History of the Former Han Dynasty* [《汉书·孔光传》], the emperor's mother granted a cane made from a tree of longevity stem to Kong Guang [孔光] (65 BCE–5 CE) the prime minister, to honor his contributions upon his retirement. The Cane of Longevity [灵寿杖], being the best type of the Elder's Cane, was considered the highest honor for an old person in ancient China.

33. Liu might have composed this poem in 809 or 810. The piece refers to planting a species in the *Atractylodes* genus. The most likely species is *bai zhu* (*Atractylodes macrocephala*). It is an herbaceous perennial that reaches roughly one to two feet tall and is native to South and Central China. For centuries, it has been used medicinally in China to treat gastrointestinal issues and other concerns.

34. The mention of "lines about planting boat orchids" alludes to the phrase in Qu Yuan's poetic masterpiece, *Li Sao* or *The Lament* [《离骚》]: "I have cultivated nine acres of orchid, and planted a hundred mu of boat orchids." In *Li Sao*, Qu Yuan complains about the king of Chu, who had dismissed Qu Yuan from his position for Qu's honest warnings. "Gathering *Osmunda* Ferns" [《采薇》] ([薇] likely referring to the fern species *Osmunda cinnamomea* L. *var asiatica*) is a poem from the *Shijing* [诗经]. This piece is about the homesickness of soldiers in border troops.

35. This line and the previous one refer to the Yongzhen Reform (805). This political movement, aiming to curb eunuchs' abuse of power, strengthen central control, punish the corrupt, and abolish excessive taxes, lasted only about six months. It ended in failure, with the emperor dethroned, the leader Wang Shuwen killed, and his assistants—including Wang Pi [王伾] (d. 806), Liu Zongyuan, and Liu Yuxi—demoted. Therefore, in these two lines Liu recalls having righted the wrongs together with his comrades and recognizes his "folly" (as some people saw it) in an ironic way. As a *sima*, an idle minor official in a prefecture, Liu Zongyuan could do nothing but take good care of himself in the remote south and try to find contentment.

36. The last two lines allude to Zhuangzi's [庄子] (roughly 369–286 BCE) essay "Know Life," [《庄子·达生》], where the stories of Shan Bao [单豹] and Zhang Yi [张毅] are told. Shan Bao leads a reclusive life, taking great care of his health, which results in a babyish rosy hue even in his seventies. However, he ends up being eaten by a tiger. Zhang Yi, in contrast, leads a social life, keen on entering all those lofty gates to establish connections with all the powerful families, but he ends up dying from exhaustion in his forties. Liu Zongyuan, demoted but still a righteous and decent man, would rather learn from Shan Bao than Zhang Yi.

37. Liu composed this poem in Yongzhou, but exactly when is unclear. Liu traveled extensively in the region.

38. Liu composed this poem in 810. Foolish Creek was the name that Liu Zongyuan gave to Ran Creek after he moved into his new house in Yongzhou. The meaning is ambiguous. The failed Yongzhen Reform (805), of which he was one of the leaders, was considered unwise by some contemporaries. In naming the creek, Liu might be admitting his "folly" in an ironic way (see note 35 to "Planting Bai Zhu" above). The name "Foolish Creek" might also allude to the legend of the Old Fool's Valley. It is said that Huan, the King of the Qi Kingdom [齐桓公] (d. 643 BCE), chased a deer into a valley. He learned from an old man that people had named the valley after the man, calling it the Old Fool's Valley. People called him the Old Fool because he sold his cow's calf for a pony, but a young man claimed the pony, saying, "a cow can never give birth to a pony" (implying the pony should not belong to the old man). Huan agreed that the old man was foolish and told the story to his prime minister, Guan Zhong, after returning to court. Guan Zhong [管仲] (723–645 BCE) realized that this story highlighted the problems with their judicial system, which had already lost legitimacy. He reformed the system, regaining the people's trust and respect. This in turn helped Huan to become the first hegemon in 681 BCE, during the Spring and Autumn period. In light of this legend, Liu's "Foolish Creek" might have implicitly satirized the problematic political system of his time, which he had tried, but failed, to reform. Regardless, the poem reveals Liu's ambivalence through the name "Foolish Creek," his acquiescence to solitude in the remote south, as well as the tension between his peaceful surroundings and his inner turmoil—an uncanny turmoil, like the "disturbing heat," that he can only relieve through loud chanting.

39. This term refers to the second of the five orders of nobility in feudal China [五等爵位], which are commonly translated (from high to low) as duke [公], marquis [侯], count [伯], viscount [子], and baron [男].

40. Liu composed this poem in 810. The last two lines allude to Fan Zhong's [樊重] story recorded in the *Book of the Later Han Dynasty* [《后汉书》] (432-445). Fan Zhong needed utensils but lacked wood to make them, so he planted catalpa and lacquer in his south garden. People laughed at him, but when they saw the trees grown up and made into utensils, they came to borrow them. Here, Liu Zongyuan uses the story as a metaphor for his planting and cultivating himself in the south, waiting to be of use again. Fan Zhong posthumously received the title Marquis of Shouzhang and the name Jing from the emperor.

41. Liu composed this poem after moving into his new house along Foolish Creek (Ran Creek) in 810.

42. Liu composed this poem in 810 or 811, after moving into his new home along Foolish Creek. Bamboo is one of the most widely depicted plants in Chinese literature and painting. For the virtues it symbolizes, see notes 9–11 to "Bitter Bamboo Bridge"; for its musical connotations, see note 49 to "Bamboo at Clear Water Courier Station."

43. This image seems to refer to a commentary in the *Yijing* or *Book of Changes* [《易经》], a text first written approximately between the eleventh and eighth centuries BCE. The line's meaning is similar to the Biblical phrase, "The spirit indeed is willing, but the flesh is weak." Our thanks to Prof. Paula Varsano for this comparison.

44. Liu might have composed this poem in 810 after moving into his new home along Foolish Creek. The piece seems to refer to a plant in the *Camellia* genus. In his essay "Flowers in T'ang Poetry: Pomegranate, Sea Pomegranate, and Mountain Pomegranate," Donald Harper hypothesizes it refers to common camellia (*Camellia japonica*). Native to Central China, Japan, and Korea, common camellia is an evergreen shrub or tree that reaches roughly ten feet tall and generally produces white, pink, or scarlet petals. It has been cultivated and appreciated in China for centuries.

45. Two of the legendary immortals' islands, said to be in the East China Sea, are called Peng and Ying.

46. Liu composed this poem in 812.

47. Liu composed this poem in 813. It allows us to infer that the previous poem, "Newly Planted Camellia," was written soon after Liu moved into his new home. For more information on camellia, see note 44 to "Newly Planted Camellia."

48. Liu composed this poem in 813. It alludes to a line from "The Song of the Three Gorges in Badong Prefecture" [《巴东三峡歌》]: "When the gibbons cry the third time, one cannot help shedding tears." Here Liu Zongyuan means, "My tears have dried up, so I can't weep when I hear the gibbons' heartbroken wails. They cry in vain."

49. Liu composed this poem in 815, on his way back to the capital, Chang'an. In Xiangyang, he and his lifelong friend the poet Liu Yuxi were invited by Zhao from Tianshui to appreciate the bamboo Zhao had planted. In the third line, "Ling Lun" [伶伦] refers to the legendary earliest official in charge of music in China, the father of Chinese music. Upon the order of the Yellow Emperor, Ling Lun made a set of tuners out of twelve bamboo pitch pipes: six imitating various sounds of a male phoenix and six those of a female. Liu might also allude to the story of Zhong Ziqi [钟子期] and Yu Boya [俞伯牙] from the Spring and Autumn period (770–221) or Warring States period. When Boya played the *guqin* [古琴] (a type of zither with seven strings), Ziqi could perceive Boya's visions of high mountains and running water. When Ziqi died, Boya destroyed his *guqin* and never played music again because he had lost his *zhiyin* [知音], or perceptive listener. Here

this poem implicitly conveys Liu's secret hope that the emperor would recognize his talents as the Yellow Emperor and Ziqi had recognized those of others.

50. Liu composed this poem in 815, during his journey from Chang'an to Liuzhou. As with many pieces, the work is both a portrait of its titular plant and a slantwise portrait of Liu. Like Liu, the pine is paradoxically punished for bringing "light" [明] (in the form of torches made from its limbs) to people. Nonetheless, it stays upright and steadfast. In Chinese culture, the pine is admired for its consistency and tenacity, which are associated with the tree's evergreen nature. The species is often depicted in Chinese literature and painting.

51. From Zhang Dunyi's [张敦颐] biographical essay, "The Political Career of Master Liu (with a Preface)" [《柳先生历官纪(并序)》] in the *Collected Works of Liu Zongyuan* [《柳宗元集》] (Beijing: Zhonghua Book Company, 1979), 1429–1434.

52. From Han Yu: "Liuzhou Luochi Temple Epitaph" [《柳州罗池庙碑》] in the *Collected Works of Liu Zongyuan* [《柳宗元集》] (Beijing: Zhonghua Book Company, 1979), 1437.

53. From Wu Wenzhi, Xie Hanqiang, ed., *The Encyclopedia of Liu Zongyuan* [柳宗元大辞典] (Hefei: Huangshan Publishing House, 2004). This book has been enormously helpful in the compiling of *The Poetic Garden of Liu Zongyuan*.

54. Liu composed this poem and the next in return for a poem from Jia Peng [贾鹏]. Jia was a hermit whom Liu befriended in Liuzhou. Jia planted pine trees around his mountain home and, delighted, he sent Liu a poem about this planting.

55. In the second month of 816, Liu witnessed a local phenomenon like that described in this poem. However, it's unclear exactly when he composed this piece. Banyan (*Ficus macrocarpa*), the species most commonly identified as [榕], is found in South China and elsewhere around the world. During the Tang Dynasty, or perhaps earlier, banyan was widely planted as a shade tree in cities throughout South China. It was considered a distinctly southern plant, and as such was included in the foundational *Plants of the Southern Regions* [《南方草木状》], traditionally attributed to the Western Jin Dynasty [西晋朝] (266–316 CE) official Ji Han [嵇含] (263–307 CE). Ji gives an extensive description of the wondrous growth patterns of the banyan tree, ending, "Southerners consider these phenomena as quite normal, and do not regard these trees as particularly auspicious."

56. Liu composed this poem in 816. As Liuzhou's prefect, he launched a reform movement to realize his ideal—"to practice the benevolent administration of Emperors Yao and Shun and Confucianism, and to bring security and prosperity to the people"—on a small scale. The reform included planting trees along streets and rivers.

57. Liu, the surname of Liu Zongyuan, means willow in Chinese; Liuzhou means Willow Prefecture. In this poem, Liu is playing with the four "Liu"s, or four "willows," namely, himself, the prefecture, the river, and the tree.

58. The "memorial tree" alludes to the story about Lord Shao [召公 or 召伯] and

the poem "Gan Tang" [《甘棠》] in the *Shijing*. Lord Shao (born before 1100 BCE), a courtier and founding father of the Zhou Dynasty, often settled disputes under a birchleaf pear tree, or Gan Tang, with wisdom and justice. After his death, people would not harm the tree because they regarded it as a memorial to him. In this poem, Liu pictures himself as being remembered in the future the way Lord Shao is remembered. But he also feels ashamed that he hasn't accomplished as much.

59. Liu composed this poem in 817. He launched a reform movement in Liuzhou, part of which was encouraging agriculture by clearing wilderness areas previously occupied by boars, snakes, and other animals. In 816, he led people to plant two hundred mandarin trees (*Citrus reticulata*) in Liuzhou's northwest corner, a newly cleared wilderness. This poem was composed the following year when Liu saw new leaves on the trees. These days, there is still a Mandarin Aroma Pavilion [柑香亭] by Liu's favorite Luochi Pond in memory of this event. Like the tangerine (also a variety of *Citrus reticulata*), the mandarin tree is native to South China, and was traditionally described as unable to bear sweet fruit in the north.

60. "That Jingzhou man" refers to Li Heng [李衡] from Jingzhou in the period of the Three Kingdoms (220–280 CE). As the Prefect of Danyang, Li had a thousand mandarin trees planted in Longyangzhou. On his deathbed, he told his son: "I have a thousand slave trees, enough for you to use." Liu did not treat the mandarin trees as his own profitable slaves (though, admittedly, they were used to benefit the local people). Instead, like Qu Yuan, Liu loved the mandarin tree and compared himself to it in terms of virtues such as loyalty and tenacity. Using plants to signify people and attributes was a longstanding practice in Classical Chinese poetry.

61. Liu composed this poem in 818, one year before his death in Liuzhou. Noble dendrobium (*Dendrobium nobile*) is an orchid species native to South China and elsewhere in Asia. It has long been used in traditional Chinese medicine, where it is given to treat a wide variety of conditions, including those related to kidneys and feet. In this poem, Liu seems to compare himself to one of the "finest blossoms" in Chang'an's Imperial Park, now cast to the "world's end" (i.e. Liuzhou). Here, Liu has nothing to do except plant noble dendrobium, a local species, in his yard. The yard and its noble dendrobium stand in contrast to the Imperial Garden and its "finest blossoms." This seems to imply Liu feels little hope of returning to the capital and fulfilling his political ambition.

Acknowledgments

We would like to thank Will Evans, Shook, Sara Balabanlilar, Walker Rutter-Bowman, Serena Reiser, the rest of the team at Deep Vellum, and Kit Schluter, without whom this book wouldn't be possible. We'd also like to thank Anhui University for its support. Special thanks to Zhao Chunqiu for permission to use his painting *Fishing Alone on the Cold River*. This book is deeply indebted to Prof. Paula Varsano, who first introduced Nathaniel to Liu Zongyuan and has provided her generous, invaluable assistance throughout the project. We are also grateful to Prof. Robert Hass for his comments on early translations, Prof. Zhou Fangzhu for the inspiration we drew from his Landscape Translation Theory, and Prof. Li Rui for her interpretation of a poem. Our thanks extend to Trisevgeni Bilia, Charles Dorfan, Prof. Ling Hon Lam, Wren Smith, and other readers for their helpful comments on the manuscript; Yu Yuanyuan's students Xia Yuting and Yang Yumeng for their literary research on Liu Zongyuan in Chinese textbooks; and Bill Porter (Red Pine), David Hinton, Sasha Dugdale, Om Anand, Joshua Krugman, Lucas McKinnon, Yan Chen, and others for thought-provoking—and fun—discussions on poetry and translation. Last, Nathaniel is grateful to Emma Leonard for her patience, encouragement, and sharp eye that helped to bring this book together, and to Jeff, Sharon, Ian, Emily, and Eli for their support. Yuanyuan's affectionate thanks extend to her family for their support.